In this story ...

Cam
(Switch)

Cam has the power to turn into animals. She is most proud of the time she stopped some baddies from robbing a bank by turning into a giraffe.

Jin
(Swoop)

Mr Trainer
(teacher)

Chapter 1: Power cut

Cam and Jin were studying in the library. Mr Trainer was going to give them a test on villains the next day.

Cam was reading a book about some of the worst villains in history. "Light Blaster fired light beams at security guards to dazzle them while he robbed banks," she read.

"It's a good job he's locked up now," Jin replied.

Light Blaster

NUMBER IN JAIL!
MOST WANTED VILLAIN

Catchphrase:
I'm having a blast!
Hobbies: collecting rare and unusual light bulbs.
Likes: fairy lights, disco balls.
Dislikes:
power cuts, water.
Beware!
Light Blaster can use light to overpower his victims.

“At least Mr Trainer defeated Light Blaster,” Jin said. “I wonder how he did it?”

“Why don’t we ask him later?” Cam replied.

Cam and Jin didn’t notice a glowing figure watching from behind a bookcase.

“Yes, I’d like to talk to Mr Trainer too … ” said the figure, softly.

Jin tried to read a couple more pages, but after a few minutes he gave up and put the book down. "We've been studying for ages," he said. "How about a game of Powerball?"

"You're on!" Cam replied.

The two friends walked to the sports hall and got a ball from the storeroom.

The rules of the game were simple: you had to kick the ball so hard it bounced off at least three walls, catch it with one hand and then hit a target.

An hour later, Cam and Jin were getting tired.

Suddenly, the lights in the sports hall flickered and went out.

"There must be a power cut," said Cam.

The emergency lights came on.

"We can still play one more game," said Jin, peering at Cam in the dim glow.

“I thought you were going to talk to Mr Trainer?” said a voice behind them.

Cam and Jin turned to see a glowing figure.

“Light Blaster!” gasped Jin.

Chapter 2: Blast battle!

Cam and Jin stared in amazement at the person standing before them.

"He looks shorter than he did in the picture," Cam whispered to Jin.

"I'll bet he's still really dangerous," Jin replied.

Cam took a deep breath and bravely stepped closer to the glowing figure. “I don’t know how you got out of jail, Light Blaster,” she said, “but you shouldn’t be here.”

“Hang on. I’m not—”

“We’re sending you back to prison!” Cam said.

Cam turned to Jin and lowered her voice. "You'd better fly out of here and raise the alarm."

Jin took off at once. He zoomed up, spun round, then headed for the door, but Light Blaster was in the way.

“Stay back!” Light Blaster warned. The emergency lights grew dimmer, and Light Blaster glowed even more fiercely.

“Look out, Jin!” Cam called. “I think he’s going to attack!”

POW! As Jin swooped over Light Blaster's head, he bounced off something invisible.

"Light Blaster must have created an energy shield," Cam thought in alarm.

Jin was flying out of control. "Oof!" He landed on a pile of crash mats.

"No!" cried Light Blaster. "That wasn't supposed to happen!"

"I suppose you hoped for something worse," said Cam angrily. "Well, you won't get away with this."

Cam became Switch and shape-shifted into an owl.

As an owl, Switch could see clearly in the dim light. With a screech, she flapped into the air.

Light Blaster turned and ran from the sports hall.

As Light Blaster raced down the corridor, the lights around him exploded. It was as if he was absorbing their energy. The energy zapped back out of him in blasts which hit the walls, lockers and windows.

Light Blaster flung open the doors and raced outside. “Keep back!” he yelled at Switch. “I don’t want to hurt you!”

A blast of energy hit a nearby tree. Switch swerved out of the way as the tree trunk cracked and fell over, almost hitting her.

Switch frowned. If Light Blaster didn't want to hurt her, why was he doing this?

The caretaker's shed exploded into splinters. Switch flew up higher to avoid the bits of wood. "I've got to stop this villain," she thought, "but how?"

Chapter 3: From dark to light

Switch swooped down towards Light Blaster.

"Keep away!" he wailed. His glowing body was starting to flicker on and off. "I've absorbed too much energy. I can't hold it in much longer. I'm dangerous!"

Switch frowned. Was he telling the truth? She flew closer to him. The hot crackle of his energy singed her wings.

Switch landed some way away and changed back into Cam. "What will happen if you release all that energy?" she called.

"It will explode in a massive blast of power," said Light Blaster. "Please, help me!"

Cam thought for a moment, then made a decision. "All right, follow me."

Cam charged across the lawn as fast as she could, back into Hero Academy. Light Blaster followed behind, being careful to keep his distance.

Inside, Cam went straight to Mrs Molten's lab, where there was a special chamber to test out all new inventions. It was made of extra-tough glass and metal.

Light Blaster ran inside, throbbing with energy. Cam pushed the door shut behind him.

Cam stared at Light Blaster helplessly. What could she do?

Just then, Mr Trainer came running in with Jin. "What on earth is going on?"

"That's Light Blaster," Jin explained.

"He's stored up too much energy," Cam said. "We have to help him!"

Crackles of light fizzed off Light Blaster and bounced off the walls of the test chamber.

Mr Trainer strode forward and turned a dial on the outside of the test chamber. “This should do it,” he said.

Cam heard a whooshing sound, like a vacuum cleaner, then some of the energy was sucked upwards into a vent.

"It's working!" Cam cried.

As more and more of the energy was drawn away, Light Blaster fell to his knees in relief.

"Who did you say that was?" Mr Trainer asked.

"It's Light Blaster. You caught him and put him in prison, remember?" Jin said.

Mr Trainer looked inside the test chamber, then frowned. “Actually I’m afraid it isn’t.”

Jin’s face fell. “What do you mean?” he asked.

“Light Blaster is still firmly behind bars. Whoever this is, it isn’t Light Blaster.”

The door to the test chamber creaked open.

“It’s true,” muttered a weak voice. “I’m not Light Blaster. I’m his son ... Blackout.”

Cam and Jin gasped.

“I share some of Dad’s powers,” Blackout explained, “but I can’t control them. I hoped that Hero Academy could help me. That’s why I sneaked in … to see what it was like.”

He looked at Cam and Jin. "I followed you two because I was hoping you'd lead me to Mr Trainer," Blackout continued. He turned to the teacher. "I thought you might be able to help me stop my powers."

"They don't need to be stopped, Blackout," said Mr Trainer.

Blackout's eyebrows shot up in surprise. "What do you mean?"

"We can help you to *control* your powers," Mr Trainer said. "If you join Hero Academy, one day, you could be a superhero."

Blackout's face broke into a wide smile. "I would love that!" he said.

“I’ll show you around,” said Cam with a grin.

Blackout looked delighted. “That would be awesome!”

“Then it’s settled,” Jin declared.

“I think you’ll do very well at Hero Academy, Blackout,” Mr Trainer said. “In fact, I’m sure you have a very *bright* future ahead of you!”